Before Therapy

Shanice Spaulding

BookLeaf Publishing

India | USA | UK

Presentation by *BookLeaf Publishing*

Web: www.bookleafpub.com

E-mail: info@bookleafpub.com

ISBN: 9789358738490

First edition 2023

I dedicate this book to my mom and my best friend Carla for always believing in me and my writing even when I didn't. This accomplishment isn't just for me, it's for us.

ACKNOWLEDGEMENT

I would like to thank everyone that inspired me to write these poems and streams of consciousness. Thank you for helping me find my passion in my darkest moments.

A series of questions everyone is too scared to ask me but I'm not scared to answer.

So does this mean that you're better because you
wrote a poem about it
Are you better because you're smiling,
                 laughing at vines again
instead of sleeping
Because you're obsessed with losing weight again?
Or because you want to go shopping, you know,
switch up your style?
Does this mean you're better because you changed
your hair?
Are you better because you're watching your favorite
movie,
or didn't cancel your coffee date with your best
friend?
Does this mean you're better because you went to
class today finally?

                              No

This means my depression still lives in me,
I smile because I'm scared of scaring my mom,

hanging out with friends so they don't know that I
still lie awake at 3 am thinking about how I wish I
wasn't   this
I went to class today because I can't get kicked out. I
also had a test that I'll probably fail anyway because I
am too sad to even pick up a textbook.
I changed my hair in hopes that someone would tell
me I look nice, sometimes I want to feel good too you
know,
I got new clothes in hopes that someone would hold
my hand and walk with me to get help
I wanted to look different to start of my road to
recovery   a new me so to speak
I'm hanging out with friends because if I wasn't I'd be
convincing myself not to walk into the nearest
hospital and tell them I don't want to be alive
anymore because it would freak my mom out,
It means my depression still lives in me and the only
thing I trust is my pen to paper or fingers to the
keyboard

What this means is that my depression is worse than
you thought,
worse than I thought but I didn't want to scare you
So instead I paint on a smile and go about the day not
worrying anyone

Catalyst

BOOM, another door is slammed shut
voices are raised and words are exchanged so
fast I can't even grasp what is happening.
It is living here I witness my first argument
between a couple, one leaving me scared,
curse words are flying back and forth, and the
yelling doesn't seem to stop
I am scared
I slowly crack open my bedroom door, tiptoeing
into the volcano still erupting
it is in this moment my entire body is engulfed
in flames as I hear the clothes rack pulled out of
the wall and shoes falling down with them
Fire spreads to the insides of my soul
This sets in motion the next 7 years of my life

Simulation

Trees sway all around me
Cars whiz past me
Laughter echoes around me
Life continues on without a second look at me

As I stand frozen in the middle
Watching all of it pass me by
This sadness has taken away so much
I'm missing so much

Plant Mom

You can not shelter something and expect it to grow beautifully. It's literally impossible. Raising a child is like growing a plant. Even if you shelter it, sure it'll grow of course, because by nature and time it will get older by a number, but it will lack everything important required to grow beautifully. I think that is where my life went wrong. I don't blame my mom either. I won't lie for a while. How could I not? It was hard watching my friends and everyone I knew do the things I couldn't. I don't mean things like sneaking out [that too] but things like making mistakes a teenager should be making, dating the wrong boy, having any experience at all with boys, quite frankly the real world. Learning from mistakes is how you grow beautifully. But I never got to make those mistakes. I'm not saying that the life I have now isn't beautiful because breathing alone is beautiful, but this isn't it. I'm stuck in this rut, not knowing how to navigate life and certain situations, not knowing what it feels like to be free, because I am a plant that was left in the shade too long.

Unrequited Love #1

There was something about the way he lights up the room the second he walks in. Illuminating the entire space with his electric smile and eagerness to talk about his unwavering faith. There was something about the way he yells when he gets excited about something, immature but like a little kid on Christmas. The look on his face when he expressed deep concern for the things he was hearing for the first time, things he could never and would never be able to understand even though I could tell he was trying his best to. Something about the amount of patience he possessed for someone that was taking forever to heal but still refused to leave my side no matter how hard I worked to push him away. How he squinted his eyes when someone says something that he disagrees with and that look of 'I'm right you're wrong' that quickly pops up on his face. The way that his laugh suffocated the entire room, especially when laughing at his own jokes. Or when he would rub his face in moments of pure frustration and tousle his hair because I said something stupid or frustrating yet again. It was the way that he didn't even notice the way people see him for more than he sees himself. How he can talk so effortlessly and with such certainty in everything he says. It was mainly about how talking to him easily became the best part of my day and he didn't even realize it. These are the things that made me fall in love with him even though I knew that the feeling would never be returned. I was just a friend. At the time it was worth it for me because just being friends was good enough. It was painful in a way that I could not recover but that was the first time I learned what it meant to have an unrequited love. But to be the first is not to be the last.

A dream is a wish

I keep having the same dream about you every night and it's
only significant because for an entire year I could never
remember my dreams and now I wish I didn't because it's
exactly that, a dream something I wish would happen and each
time I wake up, I am angry. More angrier than the day before.
Angrier than the day I told you my feelings for you never went
away and you said you weren't going to pursue anything right
now and then texted me a week later 'you're loved beyond
your comprehension, have a great day today' / Yes every time I
remember a dream I get sad, sad because it reminds me of the
day you saved me from my recurring vicious thoughts of not
wanting to exist anymore when absolutely no one else was
there for me and then two days later had the nerve to ask me if
I'm in love with you / Correct answer is yes by the way/ You
use that phrase a lot to keep me feeling crazy, because you
always have to prove that you're right/ By the way, I officially
hate those three words / Every time I remember a dream I grow
exhausted thinking of how you hold my heart in your hand like
the words it speaks was made just for you, carefully playing
the words over and over again so that you could swallow them
and regurgitate them back to me in a twisted way that fit your
narrative / Every time I remember a dream that's not all that I
remember, I remember how you conveniently don't love me
back but somehow always manage to bring it up in
conversation just enough to stroke your ego and when I ask
you why, you swear up and down that my unconditional love
for you isn't an ego boost/ Right, okay, sure / These are my
three new favorite words now because they are the only words
that I know how to say when someone is talking to me because
I am too busy remembering / Every time I remember a dream I
get frustrated / That no matter how much you have ripped my
heart apart, no matter how much you hurt me this dream of
mineis real life too because I still love you in both my dreams
and reality /

Fly Swatter/Again?

Fly Swatter

Everytime I try to reach out for help I get
swatted away like a fly
So I'm teaching myself how to bottle it up
I can feel the cap is about to pop
When it does everyone will continue to ignore
me
I'll bottle that up too
and the cycle will start all over again

Again?

It feels like I am never taken serious enough
No one listens when I talk
When they do they find any and every reason to
make it sound like no big deal
I hear them whispering 'it's just her being
dramatic again'
I keep trying to tell everyone something is
wrong
No one listens to me they think I'm the girl who
cried wolf

10

I was never allowed to stay out late, my mom
always worried something might happen
But when I bought my car there was no stopping
me
I ignored her request and hung out at night with
friends and stayed out until the world became
silent
Staying out late was something I did because I
thought it made me normal like the rest of my
friends
I was trying to fill the hole in my chest of being
so alone
It never worked, part of it was because I knew
these people didn't really care about me and
every time in the middle of the night I'd look up
at the moon
I'd feel so far away from everything
these people, this world, this life, myself
I grow quick with sadness disconnected from
everything
It is not until I hear laughter and I'm brought
back to reality
I look around at my so-called friends and they
all look unfamiliar and I want to go back home

So I go back home and wait for the next event
for the temporary relief to kick in

Lost connection

The timeline of it all is all blurry now
but what I felt for you then and now remains clear
I wanted to be with you, but I didn't know how
you wanted to be with me, but didn't know how
we both labeled failed attempts of us being together
with us being just being "weird"
but then I stopped being weird and I wanted us to work
and suddenly you're no longer acting weird but distant
I want to be with you but you've moved on
you stopped being weird for someone else
you're giving someone else everything you said you couldn't
give me because you were too weird
I am being slapped in the face everyday watching you treat
someone else better,
as I watch it all unfold one lie in particular stands out that you
said
"I'm not going anywhere Shanice, I want us to work"
so why did you walk away without even a glance back
why did you fight so hard in the first place
to stop suddenly
Was it not enough? Was the pace too slow? Was it because I
was scared that you would hurt me? Is it because you never
liked me? Was it because I was right, that you did hurt me?
or did you grow tired of waiting on me like everyone else?
maybe I took what you said too literally and dragged it out for
too long but
I'm sorry I couldn't jump into a relationship right away like
you asked me in the beginning
You didn't even say goodbye or anything
You lied to me about her and I had to pull it out of you
yet suddenly waves of missing you are hitting me harder than
ever and
Everyday I have to convince myself that I dodged a bullet with
you

Hands

My hands are stronger than my heart and brain
combined together
It sounds unbelievable but it's true hear me out
My hands have done a lot for me
They've wiped the tears from my face so I could
face the world again
They've pushed against my mattress getting me
out of bed when my own brain told me to lay
there all day
Thanked my best friend with hugs when my
brain suddenly forgot how to say "thank you"
but remembered to say thank you to my broken
heart instead because the pain always reminds
me that I'm still alive
Most importantly my hands have showed me
there's a way to express my self that's not
beating myself up
My hands tell me that everything will be okay
when every other part of my body says I'm
dying

Accepting trauma

They say your childhood years shape you for your teenage years and your teenage years shape you for adulthood and then it's off you go into the real world but what do you do when those primal times were jam-packed with trauma and it's adulthood and you don't know what the hell is going on?

Unrequited Love #2

I want to hold your hand countdown

1. It's dark and I check the time on my phone almost blinding myself
with the brightness
I'm shocked at how late it is, time with you always seemed to go too
fast and never lasted long enough. I'm laying on your bed and you're
sitting on the floor and we've been watching this show for hours. You
rest your arm on the end of your bed and at this point I've lost interest
in the show, I am staring at your hand and all I want to do is reach out
and hold it, time stops and that's all I can think about. What it would be
like to hand in hand with you, in sync. That feeling sticks with me the
rest of the night
2. We are in the car driving, I can't remember if it was to or from the
museum, I get so lost in your words sometimes losing track of
everything else. I remember you were telling me a story about how you
made plans to hook up with this one girl but you didn't go through with
it. I remember that story ended with you saying how you just wanted to
hold hands with someone. My knuckles turn white I am gripping the
steering wheel so hard and it's the first time in the entire car ride I have
no response to what you said. How can I respond when the only thing I
wanted to do at that moment was to grab your hand.
3. The night is finally over and we are standing around the exit trying to
leave but it's overcrowded with people so leaving is a difficult task.
You're standing in front of me and I start to drift off in thought, finally
calm from the panic attack I had 5 minutes prior. Did you know being
overwhelmed with love for someone can actually cause you to panic,
anyways I'm about to answer that thought in my head when you grab
my hand and you start pushing through the crowds of people with ease
and finally we make it outside of the building greeted with the crisp hot
air. You Let go of my hand and it feels like a part of me is missing now.
I mumble "that was annoying" and you say sorry that you were just
trying to get us out and I am quick to reassure you I meant the crowd of
people was annoying not you holding my hand. It is the first and the
last time I will ever know what it's like to be hand in hand with you
even if our palms were sweaty and it was completely innocent. It's
something I will grow to crave for what feels like an eternity. I still
want to hold your hand

Starving Writer

Food has always been a struggle for me
for years it was the only thing that comforted me
and in return I gained a lot of weight
but then I looked around and saw how skinny my
friends were and grew sad
the resentment all the way to my lack of self-control
increased
especially when mom told me everyday how big I was
so I lost majority of the weight and felt confused when I
didn't feel any better
I was skinnier with no comfort

Going forward mom made sure to question if I went
back for seconds at dinner
making me feel like that overweight girl again

Now things have progressively gotten worse but it is
more intense and obsessive this time
I'm battling with food again
my body is crying out for nutrients but
I'm restricting my meals and
eating too much today to punish my body the next

I don't want mom to get mad again
and I don't want to gain weight

but they don't tell you that the most satisfying thrill is
punishing yourself knowing you will be skinny again.

Dirty clothes

Folding clothes means I'm doing okay again
it means instead of staying in the same hoodies
for days on end questioning why am I still alive,
I'm questioning what the future has planned for
me. You see, clean clothes mean I put effort into
my appearance not for you or him or her but for
me. Because I feel life in me again and I feel
like I want to share that life with the world.
You see when the laundry basket contains less
dirty clothes than the week before it means that
I've only found refuge in my hoodie all week
because it's the only thing that has come to bring
me comfort lately, the only consistent
but when my towel has managed to make it into
the laundry basket it means that my mood
swings are subtle and I feel good again
it means that even though I've slipped into
isolation and loneliness
I still remember to shower.
The laundry basket is full this week and my
clothes are happy to be dirty again.

Pain

Pain has a nasty familiarity to it
I always hate when the feeling comes back
not that it ever really left
It's always sitting there even in the background
waiting just for me
pretending that it's gone
and just as I think I can stand, pain breaks my
legs again and I fall to the floor
Pain has always been there for me when
everything and everyone else failed
pain is all I have left
Pain reminds me that I'm still here even if I'm
crumbling
Pain whispers in my ears everyday
at school, at work, in the shower, right before
bed
pain is always here to remind me that no one
wants damaged goods and that no matter how
hard I try to exchange these damaged goods for
something brand new
no one will want them and I'm stuck with this
pain forever crippling me

A funeral

People dressed in black with tear-stained faces
they each stop to hug my mom and pass along a "I'm so sorry
for your loss"
Some will even try saying "she was such an amazing person"
but no one will say which knife in my back has their name on
it
How could they there's so many I've even lost track
They'll all say "If only I knew"
even though a majority of them stopped being my friend
because I was too sad or didn't like me because of it
The service will continue and the pastor will read out a bible
verse, the one about blessing my soul and my mom will sit
front row the most hurt but one of the least understanding of
how depressed I was,
It's okay, I knew that it was hard to grasp that I wasn't just
depressed it was so much more
the mic will be handed over to those who want to speak and
surprisingly so many people come up and have so much to say
about how I had such great character, I was such a good friend,
I was beautiful and I had so much to offer the world
if there is an afterlife I'm laughing now because I've never
heard any of this before in fact it's always been silence from
everyone
the service ends and as I'm lowered 6ft under people really
start to lose it crying so hard yelling "why"
It's all a performance
the day will come to an end and everyone will go home
they'll post about me for a day or so
and then everyone's true colors show and I'm never once
thought of again just like How I never was in this life
and finally when the last thought is thought of me
I'll be able to rest in peace because I always knew
in life and in death I was never missed

A funeral part 2

Or maybe I'm right and no one will show up because no one cared

Phoenix rising

I like baths that are too hot. Turn the water to the highest setting. Watching the water rise higher and higher. Half a bag of epsom salt in. Eucalyptus engulfed my nose. I dip my right toe in. Scorching hot but I can't give up. I dunk my whole foot in and then bring my left in next. My feet are burning but it's nothing compared to the burning desire for someone, anyone to tell me they love me, that they are proud of me, maybe beautiful even. I don't push it but I push the rest of my body in the water. My whole body is on fire. The first thing to accurately match what I feel on the inside daily. I can't think. The water is too hot. That's the point. I don't want to think about anything. I'm focusing on my heartbeat, it's going so fast. I can hear it in my ears. It's begging me to get out. To breathe. I'm out of breath now. I plunge my body deeper. I have forgotten everything. I'm focusing on the sweat dripping down my face. This is good. Sweat it out. As if it were that easy. I think I'm visiting life for the first time. I jump up from the water gasping for air. I'm greeted with death again. The death of so many things that I've failed at in life. But it's okay, I like baths now. I like pretending that I'm living life and not death.

Little girl

I miss the younger me, when I used to sit in the corner everywhere I went, reading. No matter the time or place, I was always buried deep in a book. That was before I made my first friend and had my first sleepover. Growing up my mom was really overprotective and looking back I guess she just didn't want to see me hurt. Because people can hurt you so much like it's nothing, but ten years later and I can't turn back from my first sleepover, I can't turn back from the first of many disappointments. I want to bury myself in so many books again, go back to that little girl who didn't know that those closest to you have the power to hurt you the most.

Can you hear me?

finding gaps in everyone's words
and I'm slowly sinking, wasting away
I've never felt so alone before; so cheated
cheated out of what I give to the world
to get pain in return
God, I am so miserably sad
I'm sad
                I'm sad I'm sad
I'm sad
      I'm sad!
                                      I'm sad
I want to cry! I want to SOB! sob so loud my
screams are forever etched into everyone's memory
I WANT MY PAIN AND MY HURT TO BE FUCKING
HEARD FOR ONCE IN MY LIFE SOMEONE PLEASE
   please
listen to me; I am dying.
I want to release at least some of this,
this heavy weight on my shoulders
but nothing will come out,
as if my body has no water left
a choked scream for help escapes me
it's so faint it can not be heard
not from those next to me, not from those far away
not from me, not from anyone,
I am alone in this life
I am alone simply forever
dear god please let me cry, my body is begging for it
begging to show that I am not all destruction
the cries rattle in me
I keep this far away dazed face on though because
no one can be bothered by me or my shit anymore
hell
I can't even be bothered with myself anymore
I want to collapse into the nothingness that has a
hold on my throat, I want to scream, kick, and punch
everything. I want to throw a temper tantrum
because I am so ANGRY, but that's frowned upon

So I'll just sit and wait as one question repeats over
Why is everything like this?

Love

Love. I want someone to be proud to call me theirs. I want all of the cute domestic shit too. I want to cook for someone I call 'my love'. I want to stay up late in bed talking about everything and anything. Skin on skin contact. God I think that's what I desire the most. Tracing fingers against my lover's skin, kissing imperfections. I want to bake brownies at 3am and then snuggle back in bed eating all of them way too fast while watching 'our' show. I want to shower together, washing each other. Laughing. Vulnerability. I want to know about my partner's past, I want to learn what makes them who they are. I want late afternoons napping on the couch together, their head laying on my chest or vice versa. I want to hold hands while grocery shopping and putting their favorite snacks in the cart because I know it's their favorite. I want to dance in our underwear until 1am and share music we think each other would like. I want to show my love off to the world, people sick of hearing me but knowing how happy I am. I want communication so strong and understanding that I feel safe. God, I want to feel safe. Safe to tell them things that scare me. I want a love where I can be me, all of me and still be loved unconditionally. I want surprises and to surprise my love with flowers, random dates and gifts I know they would like. I want kisses everywhere. I want a love that I don't have to question because I always feel it. I want to love someone with all of me and someone to love me with all of them. Love.